Starting & Running

Your Own

Business.

First Published in 1975 by

MOORE PUBLISHING
ABACUS HOUSE
GRIMSBY DN31 3PD

ISBN 0 904823 00 8

Printed in Great Britain by Elsworth Brothers Ltd.

STARTING YOUR OWN

BUSINESS —

a blueprint for success

Golden Rules, Golden Advice, and Golden Checklists.

Alvin Taylor

BUSINESS IS PEOPLE.
If you're no good at the people business —
You'll be no good as a business person.

List of Contents.

Preface

Welcome to Our World.

It's very easy to be independent — to be your own man.
Just quit your job.

But, do I hear you say, what about the mortgage, rent, food?
Right! Of course it's easy to be independent — but to be
successful you have to **do the job right.**

And that's what this material is all about. So if you'd like to
join — read the material, learn the golden rules, follow the
golden advice and use the golden checklists.

They're based on sound successful experience and many
mistakes.

And they're yours to use as you please.

After that **IT'S UP TO YOU.**

Introduction

In November 1972 I decided to open my own retail business. Fifteen months later I had made ten times my former annual income from a business which only existed ten months.

In the five months I was busy "getting the business together," I read many business books, none of which really filled the burning need I had for information to help me do the job. So I did it the hard way. By bitter experience.

How I did it you will find within the covers of this book.

My objective in writing this book was to produce a primer to help other newcomers to their own business, covering all those problems which I had to overcome in my early days, and anticipating other problems which could have arisen had I been less lucky.

The style used is straight from the shoulder with no words wasted, because when you are planning a business venture you have no time for irrelevancies.

Your objective, I imagine, in acquiring the book is to prepare yourself for running your own business, or help you improve your current one.

By making the investment you have taken the first step towards a new you, a new future and possibly undreamed of wealth. And I wish you well.

But before you start, just one thought. Your decision to buy this book was a positive one. When you read this book remain of positive mind. Then acquire your business and run it in a positive manner. But if you feel, having read the book that you are insufficiently prepared to run your own business yet, but still want to do so, then make a positive decision not to take any further action for three months (except reading books on business).

When the three months are up come back to the book, read it afresh, again in a positive manner. You will find that either you are now ready — or the will to do it has diminished — make your own decision.

But all the time you have your own business in mind you owe it to yourself and those about you, to think. To Think Big, TO THINK POSITIVE.

1 What shall I do?

Golden Rule: Know Your Own Subject.

Make your business something you already know a lot about.
Maybe it's very close to your present job.

Perhaps you've noticed that your own job, or company would function more efficiently by the provision of a new service. Could you provide that service? Perhaps you work for a company where retail outlets for **your type** of products (not just your company's products) are insufficient. Could you open and run a shop?

Perhaps, as a former colleague did, you are certain that a market exists for products which you are accustomed to making, in different forms (cheaper, more expensive, smaller, larger, bluer, brighter, circular, square, in pairs, in plastic, in metal etc. etc.). Are you capable of developing, making and marketing these products?

Maybe, as two very different friends did, you feel that you can set up in competition with your current employer by doing a better job or offering the customer a better deal. (One has four retail chemist shops, the other, one of London's fastest growing and most successful advertising agencies).

Possibly you could convert one of your company's waste by-products into a useful and saleable item (do ensure continuity of supply before committing yourself to such a venture).

You could set up in a totally unfamiliar field, but this can prove dangerous, if not disastrous.

You can be sure that you will make a lot of mistakes, even if you are playing on your own ground — because a lot of the tasks you have to tackle will be new to you.

You will do well to eliminate as many unknowns as possible before you start.

If however you do decide to set up in a totally fresh field do not be 'sold' the idea and start off on a cloud of hot air and enthusiasm. Consider the prospects very seriously and keep asking yourself, what, if I pursue this course of action, is the worst thing that can happen? And if it looks at all gloomy, think again.

It would be wise at this point also to advise you never to take anyone's promise in business unless you have it in writing, or better still with the back-up of a legal agreement which your solicitor should vet for you. There are too many cases of verbal misunderstandings in business which could easily be avoided by the simple expedient of putting pen to paper.

Golden Advice: Beware of setting up in price competition with a business with fat profits or easily prunable overheads! The business may be structured to take account of potential competition and will probably price you out of the market (perhaps out of reserves).

2 A Place for Everything, and Everything in its Own Place.

Golden Rule: Take advantage of the opportunities as they arise.

Sorry. The headline is misleading, and deliberately so — because you might as well know right now; **There is no set order for doing things.** — even when you're getting started.

You might get the staff first, or the premises, or the customers, and so you'll find this happening as you go along. **So be prepared** and you'll succeed.

My order for doing things was probably the most usual in opening a retail company. The idea, followed by the premises, ordering stock, premises made ready, appointing staff, stock into shop. Advertising closely followed, I'm delighted to say, by the customers.

However there are many other methods of getting started. One often quoted is the entrepreneur with no capital who goes along to the bank and asks for a loan against his only collateral, a sheaf of firm orders for the product or service he plans to provide. That, I would suggest, is an apocryphal story, and although it may happen, I for one wouldn't like to try it. You'd need to visit just about every bank in a city the size of Glasgow before you'd be sure of getting sufficient support for such an idea (but don't try Glasgow — Glaswegians are awfully shrewd when it comes to money). If the entrepreneur would put his house and car up as additional security he'd be on a firmer wicket. But it isn't only at the beginning that you need to **be prepared.** To start a business you need guts and a good idea, to keep it running successfully from day to day you need to be pretty cute too.

Golden Advice: If you can see ahead of you, events which could radically affect the course of your business, prepare contingency plans, before the pressure is on.

3 Attitude of Mind.

Golden Rule: If you are not prepared for total committal, do not commit yourself at all.

Your reasons for wanting to start your own business must be valid ones. Otherwise you will start out with the wrong attitude of mind — and fail.

Four good reasons for starting your own business.
    1: You feel under-employed.
    2: You have seen a need which can be exploited.
    3: You feel you will enjoy taking all the final decisions.
    4: You enjoy what you're doing now, but would prefer total involvement.

Four bad reasons for starting your own business.
    1: Your employer expects you to,
        a) Work too long.
        b) Work for too little pay.
        c) Do things which you weren't originally expected to do.
    2: Being your own boss means nobody will tell you what to do.
    3: You think self employment = semi retirement.
    4: You are redundant and finding a job at your age will be difficult.

You should be prepared to learn the economic facts of life. The world is extremely competitive and you will be out there, like an orphan in the storm, with very few friends and probably many enemies, worried that you might take the bread from their mouths.

Unless you have, in physical terms, a big heart, a broad back, a strong stomach and a double measure of resilience you should forget the idea altogether.

The road to success will be fraught with many setbacks.

4

Some of the most successful business enterprises have at some time been in such a position that liquidation has appeared more sensible than carrying on.

Golden Advice: Persistence is its own reward (but only if the graph is on an upward trend!).

4 You Need Friends.

Golden Rule: Pick associates whose speciality will help you and your problem.

The late Gerald Nabarro — a self made man — said that a businessman's best friends are, his bank manager, accountant, lawyer and tailor— and while I'd take issue with him on the tailor, he may be right — he was certainly more successful than I have been to date.

These are the sort of friends you need, and you must pick them very carefully. They must be people who will take a personal interest in **you**.

How to find them? Talk to people who can advise you on this problem, and lots of other things too.

There really is a lot of advice available. Some of it good — some bad — (well it had to get difficult some time) — your task is to decide on the value of that advice.

Free advice available here.
Bank managers.
Building society managers. } and their staff.
Business transfer agent.
Advertising agencies.
Local traders.
Similar businesses, different areas.
Personal friends.
Estate agents.
Local newspaper (particularly Advertising Managers).
Libraries.
What kind of advice can you get?

Bank managers can put you onto solicitors and accountants, they spend their life working with them.

Building societies can also help you here, and although their speciality is residential property, they can indicate property values, and advise you where to seek further advice.

Business transfer agents in particular know the banks, and accountants who will support small traders, and give them the kind of service they need.

Advertising agencies have a wealth of superficial experience in many areas, don't expect any depth from their advice until you start paying for it (even then it probably won't amount to much) but do listen, for you'll find many a pearl among the stones.

Local traders (providing that you're not competing with them) can tell you whose services they find acceptable, from solicitors to linen service.

Personal friends may contribute very little, but their thoughts may act as catalysts to your own and help you get your thinking straight.

Parallel traders in other areas and Estate Agents can offer you very obvious advice.

Local newspapers can help you two ways. Firstly there's the files of old newspapers, which can paint a picture of recent history, also picking out the advertising will show you how active the competition has been in the past.

Old history is, however, of little value, and you are recommended not to waste your time on it.

Advertising managers can advise you on local trading conditions, and while it is not ethical to name names in such discussions the advertising manager is generally unable to hide identities in the course of such discussions.

Libraries have notice boards which are littered with the latest information on what are fundamentally purely local events. But if what you are looking for is not there do not lose heart. Ask the librarian in a quiet moment. My own experience is that this profession falls into the category of world's most helpful people — even if they do only talk in whispers.

A couple of Golden Warnings here though.

1) Always take advice in which the informer has a vested interest with a large dollop of salt.

2) Beware of people like a certain Josh Billings who graced this planet in the 19th Century, and is reputed to have said "When a man comes to me for advice, I find out the kind of advice he wants, and I give it to him." Cynical old sages like that are best left in the nineteenth century.

Golden Advice, on Advice.

Weigh it very carefully.

5(a) What your Supporters Need to Know.

Golden Rule: Have a plan and monitor your progress against it as often as you can.

Your supporters need to know what you plan to do.

So you'd better put it down in writing. What they really want to know is, 'how much money do you plan to make.'

Now the thing to remember is that this is only your **plan**.

What actually happens to your business against the plan doesn't matter all that much, providing that you take the appropriate action.

In other words — if it's obvious you've backed a loser you get out soon enough to save your bacon — or if you are being more successful than you planned you raise more cash and recruit more personnel to back the expansion.

I find the best way to monitor against plan is on a moving-total graph against parameters of sales, gross margins and overheads.

Initially this should be done on a weekly basis, the fact that the total is moving (say 3 or 4 weekly) smoothes out the humps to give a clear picture of the direction of the business.

The **sales graph** is only a guide.

You **will** know your business is heading for success if your **gross margin** is moving ahead of **overheads.** Your prediction should allow for any seasonality in your business pattern. Incidentally if you find that things are not going as planned, take whatever remedial action you feel appropriate and if this is unsuccessful do not be afraid to take a loss, and sell out or give up.

No one will thank you for postponing the inevitable, not your customers, your suppliers or your family.

Golden Advice: If at first you don't succeed try, try again. Then quit. No use being a damn fool about it (W. C. Fields) — funny — but true.

5 (b) Sample Business Plan.

A Wellington Boot Supermarket For Manchester.

Background: It is planned to open a specialist wellington boot retail supermarket in Lower King Street, Manchester.

The location has been selected because,
1: It is a basement, with low rent, and no window space is thought necessary.
2: There is a tremendous "passing trade."
3: It is commodious, and will allow large displays.
4: It rains a lot in Manchester.

(Comment: Three of the four above are the sort of realistic perameters which you must adopt when selecting a location. Your background need not include location — in fact you may write your plan without a location but include a target location).

The attached plan
1: Objectives.
2: Marketing platform.
3: Growth prospects / plans.
4: Problems.
5: Finance.
6: Net profit trading forecast. September 1975 — August 1976.

(Comment: No other headings need be included in such a plan. However should you require in depth financing, you must be prepared to answer some very searching questions on your plans.

Vague assurances or "pie in the sky" will not suffice for such an important topic).

Objectives.
a) To earn £4,000 in year one.
b) To sustain and maintain a minimum growth rate of 25% p.a.
c) To achieve a minimum return on capital of 30% (after drawing a working wage).

(Comment: These are all reasonable figures, though now it is becoming common to exclude inflation from item (b) and aim for a lower growth rate to add to inflation).

Operating Objectives.
a) To buy at best trading terms where possible.
b) To take settlement discount where offered.
c) To have the largest range of wellington boots in any shop in Britain.
d) To make special offers by buying ex-mail order job - lots
e) To earn an average gross margin of 40% (note this is high).
f) To offer genuine / expert sales advice.
g) To recruit and train staff for growth.

(Comment: The operating objectives describe how you plan to achieve your prime objectives and give background to your thinking on how you will run the operation. It is here that the plan becomes an excellent discipline in helping you become clear in your own mind exactly what you plan to do. Having stated these objectives you can ask yourself how will you do it? How will I handle point (f) and offer genuine and expert sales advice? Will I send my staff on courses? — or train them myself? — or employ pretrained experts?).

Marketing Platform.
"The biggest choice at the best prices."
Choice.
Brands: The best from Britain, America and New Zealand.

Quantity: The biggest in any single shop in the north of England.

Availability: Laid out for all to see samples. Spacious fitting accommodation.

Payment Methods: Cash, Cheque, Barclaycard, Access, Trading checks.

Shopping Times: Monday, Tuesday, Wednesday, 9.00 - 6.00.
Thursday,   8.30 - 6.30.
Friday,   8.30 - 7.30.
Saturday,   8.30 - 6.00.

Guarantees.
  (1) Not to let water in for 12 months.
  (2) To retain original colour for 6 months.
  (3) Money back or free replacement if dissatisfied within guarantee period.

(Comment: If our platform is one of choice we must show that we have choice not only of the best boots or best brands, but also of payment method, long shopping hours and back this with understandable and useful guarantees.

We have also indicated that the pricing philosophy will be keen — this must be on the mail-order specials since we have already indicated that we will be aiming for a high margin).

Growth Prospects / Plans.

The wellington boot market is one of slow growth and limited prospects. However it's lack of "glamour" means that it is one of little competition and therefore high margins can be earned.

Our "pitch" is on choice, and we feel that we can only offer growth in other large towns such as Liverpool, Leeds, Birmingham, Glasgow and Edinburgh.

No actual plans for growth can be put forward until June. First it is necessary to determine just how successful unit one is.

(Comment: This looks rather gloomy, but at least we can be said to be realistic (and any other plan isn't worth the paper it's written on). What is important is the final paragraph. With a new business you cannot plan unit 2 until you know how well unit 1 is going. What could be possible though is to expand within the same building into either sports shoes, or more likely from a sales point of view (though with different buying expertise requirement), umbrellas and / or rainwear. Any such thoughts should be included in the plan).

Problems.

We see our only substantial problem one of obtaining supplies, as the industry is currently production limited. However as we have a knowledge of the industry we feel we shall be able to overcome the problem.

(Comment: Any business that only foresees one problem — which it has already overcome, is doomed to failure. The writer of the plan is being super-optimistic.

When you do your plan, consider very carefully the competition, and specifically what action it may take when you arrive on the scene. Also no business sits still, what may they be doing now?

How will the planner get people to go down to a basement in a medium traffic area?

What sort of people buy wellies from basements?

How will stock move in and out if there is only one door?

Have we considered the possibility of a flood in the basement?

This area of your plan should be the most carefully thought out, if not spelt out. When your bank manager sees it he will be asking you "What thoughts have you given to xxxxxxx?" Invariably he will refer to what could be a problem. Rise to the occasion — otherwise he might think you got your plan out of a book . . . .).

Finance.

We are able to inject £9,000 without obtaining outside finance.

Initial Business Outgoings.

Fixtures and fittings	..	..	..	800
Lease and legal	..	..	..	..	475
Advertising	..	..	..	..	..	1,000
General other	..	..	..	..	125
				2.400

Available for stock, working capital etc.   £6.600

(Comment: In that case the planner may need a bank loan. The figures overleaf show that £6,600 buys 14 weeks stock, and when you are offering the best choice in the North of England this is probably insufficient particularly in the first instance when the business has to buy all it's display samples, and a selection of lines which will be necessarily slow moving).

Net Profit Trading Forecast.

Sept. 1 1975 — Aug. 31 1976.

Outgoings.

Rent	1.400
Rates	500
Staff	2,700
Drawings	4,000
Vehicle	800
Power	250
N.I. etc...	400
* Advertising	1,100
General..	300
	11,450

* Not including launch.

Sales Forecast.

Sales	37,000
Margin 40%	14,800
Less outgoings	11,450
Net Profit	3,350

Total net profit £3,350 = 37% return on capital employed (£9.000).

(Comment: All interested parties now have some figures into which they can sink their various teeth and judge whether they will be able to act for and with the proposed new business man (or lady).

The bank in particular if it agrees to overdraft facilities will be particularly anxious to follow the progress of the business against this plan, certainly in it's early days).

6 Selecting the Premises.

Whatever your line of business, you must have somewhere to carry it out.

We're on to a very important decision now. If your business is not something you can easily do at home, you are about to commit **An Expenditure.**

Two Golden Rules — Whether you lease or buy.
1) Obtain a property you can equally easily dispose of.
2) Select the least expensive accommodation that will do the job adequately.

And a Piece of Golden Advice.

If you are not at all sure that the premises are right for the job, or good value, **or anything**, employ a specialist — A business or property consultant whose track record is known to you, or your solicitor, accountant or bank manager. If he confirms your opinion you can be reasonably confident of your choice, if he tells you it's "no go" your money on his fee is well spent.

A lease commits you to pay rent on a property for a definite period, so if the worst happens and your business is not a success the last thing you want is an expensive lease round your neck.

So whether you like it or not you are in the property business. You might as well get into the fastest appreciating asset which will serve your business well.

Now Some Golden Clues— for Retail Property.

(1) **Look for secure areas.** — where whatever happens, property will probably maintain it's value (like next door to Marks and Spencer, Boots and W. H. Smiths). This however may prove rather expensive for you and you may like to look for;

(2) A "Coming Area." These may be found;

a) In just off the High Street sites, where property is available but currently unused, and where there is not a superfluity of other similar property.

b) In town centres which are being rapidly re-developed. (Successful businesses may have to move while their own site is being re-developed).

c) In areas where businesses are successful, but not yet modernised. (Shopfront modernisation to a complete street can as much as double the passing trade).

d) On main "through routes." Often you find a town commercial (banking) centre is between two shopping areas. Commercial centres tend to charge office and showroom rent which is lower than shop rent.

Other good sites may be between any of the following points. Railway Station, Bus Station, Football Ground (could be dangerous) Department Store, Theatre / Cinema / Bingo Club, Major Car Park, Town Hall.

Another "coming area" may be where a "star" draw is about to establish itself (again like the market leaders such as W. H. Smiths). However a specialised store such as Mothercare, or Hepworths Menswear may have a better "rub off" for your own type of trade, (or market) which may be young mothers or middle market males. etc.

Golden Clues for Manufacturers.

The problems here, though different, are similar although now you are not looking for an area where you can attract customers, but workers — and just as you wouldn't put the most expensive glass and china shop in the roughest neighbourhood in town, neither would you put a manufacturing plant requiring a patient and delicate handwork operation in an area where the only free labour is a group of say, miners who have recently been laid off because the seam has run out. (If, however, their wives are looking for work, this could be your golden opportunity).

Some former colleagues of mine located in an area of underemployment for lady process workers, who had previously worked at a local woollen mill. They took over the most modern extension to the mill and got it for a chorus of the proverbial song. Now the ladies are happily making a light engineering product where previously they did something to wool.

The premises in this case provided not only the space in which to work, but also the labour force.

Special Golden Advice.

Do not locate in an area where there is much competition for the type of labour you require. You will find that big companies will always pull the best staff, if not through the money they offer, through the advantages of their social clubs and schemes. You'll probably get the staff alright — all the ones the major company already fired.

General.

How to find the right areas.

    (1) **Talk to people.**
    a) Estate agents.
    b) Business transfer agents.
    c) Window cleaners (don't laugh — I'm still learning everytime I talk to mine). They can tell you when a company is moving out. One of the first things they do is stop cleaning windows. They can also tell you when an unoccupied property is to be occupied, as the first thing the new owner does is get it cleaned up.

    (2) **Don't be an armchair shopper.**
    a) Walk round likely town centres.
    b) Drive to likely shopping parades and industrial estates.
    c) Ring, or best of all, visit every single estate agent with a board up. Don't just write. You learn so much by talking to people.

As a side issue.

One of your most important assets as a business man will be you and your voice. I know plenty of successful people, but I can't think of one who is a **self made success** who is an inadequate oral communicator. If this is a weaker weapon in your armoury may I suggest that you take urgent steps to work on this aspect of your make-up.

7 Selecting and Rewarding Staff

No Golden Rules here, just a Golden Warning, Be Very Very Careful.

Your business, whatever it is, will hinge on people, people making, selling or accounting on your behalf.

Before you decide to employ someone, be very certain that you know;

1) What the job is.

2) What personal attributes the person must therefore have. Also be sure that before you employ someone, he knows what the job is and exactly what you expect of him, and what will happen if he fails you.

I heard a story recently about a man who was appointed to a position in overall charge of a company, reporting to the board of a parent company. When he arrived to do the job he found that while he had been given the responsibility, he had not been given the authority as two other people within the company also reported to the board of the parent company. A strange sort of affair, but the really inexcusable factor was that the man left the interview and accepted the job on a completely fallacious understanding.

The lesson to learn is that if it can happen in a large, successful, company, it can happen to you too.

In terms of required performance, you should be very demanding and remember **no one** should match up to your demanding requirements — if someone does, ask yourself

"Am I demanding enough."

Golden Advice: If you value your staff highly (i.e. their departure would require replacement by a person who would require intensive training) — overpay them. If, however, your staff can be relatively easily replaced then every £ you overpay is a £ out of your pocket.

8 The Pressures you are Likely to Face (Workload).

If your business is at all successful you will from time to time find yourself, and eventually your workforce subject to the most intolerable workload. Most business books advise you to ensure that you never recruit new staff until everyone in the business is so overworked that they welcome anyone, but, anyone.

It's horses for courses, and on occasion I'd subscribe to this view. But most business books assume a perfect world — don't forget if everyone in the business does get violently overworked the following could happen;

1) They might quit for a slightly quieter life.
2) Mistakes could happen, and go unnoticed for some time.
3) Somebody might feel overexploited and sabotage the effort, or agitate with other workers for better pay / conditions.
4) People fall ill much easier.

Our Golden Rule for this section must be to make sure that you: Don't let the business run you.

If the work load becomes too great, you'll find yourself "putting out fires" all the time, instead of planning for the future.

It is essential that you **legislate against any crisis that occurs more than once,** so that someone else at a lower level is able to handle this without reference to you.

This will then allow you to get on with your job which will include planning work, and the progress of the business (and what would they do if you were away).

Golden Advice: Make sure that as soon as your business becomes profitable you can leave it for two weeks holiday (you don't have to go — just ensure you can if you want to).

9 Delegation and Reponsibility.

Golden Rule: If you want to delegate work, you must delegate most of the responsiblity that goes with it.

If you've picked the right people and you want to have a business that grows BIG, you'd better start delegating yourself out of a job.

To do this you must shed real responsibility, so that your people become achievers, not just doers.

You set the ground rules, and keep a watchful eye over the proceedings, but that's all.

Let your people learn to run the business your way, then you can devote your talents to something you've become rather clever at — starting a new business.

Too often one hears of companies where the person who created the successful company simply refuses to let go of the reins. The net result of such an action is that the head of the company becomes overworked, and probably pretty intolerable to work with. The staff that he employs will be second raters, either because they are potential first raters and he has stifled their growth, or more likely any real talent has left the company for a brighter and better tomorrow elsewhere. And when the time comes for the head to retire — or develop his business there's just no one in the middle management strata to take over.

So far we've only talked about good employees — the winners — what about the losers? The not so good ones.

Golden Advice: If you picked a wrong person as an employee, don't compound the error.

Regard it as dutch elm disease, which can destroy all around it — and fire the offender.

10 How to Expand.

Golden Rule: Expand with caution.

It's a funny thing, but many people who are good at starting businesses are pretty awful when it comes to real expansion. This is often because they try to repeat a previous action. This is generally wrong, because circumstances and time change the consequence of the action.

However expansion is really rather easy, for if you retain your flexibility, you only need two things to help you expand.

People and Money. After all you already have the idea, and an indication of possible market potential.

We have already indicated that you should delegate work and responsibility, encouraging training by doing. Your staff should be encouraged to use the same method of working, so that they might grow into the new positions you will be creating.

An example of this method of training in a new **industry** dates back to the 1760's / 1780's when it worked very well for an engineer James Brindley. Brindley having built the first major canal in Britain for the Duke of Bridgewater was called upon to engineer many more. Brindley accepted many consultancy contracts and put in assistants who he more or less left to it. These men were experienced engineers, but with little or no canal experience (there were so few canals), Brindley called on them occasionally and they were able to consult with him if the need arose.

This method of work and training does sometimes cause displeasure amongst those being trained — I've experienced it myself, one feels one is doing all the work and getting none of the kudos, or more importantly the brass. As one of the Brindleys assistants said at the time "My master Brindley never paid half the attention to all the canals he was concerned in as I pay to this single one; he neither set out the work or measured it as I measured it, yet he received near £2,000 a year".*

The moral is perhaps to set the example of hard work. Read what Bill Gold of Washington Post and Times Herald has to say "I've met a few people in my time who were enthusiastic about hard work. And it was just my luck that all of them happened to be men I was working for at the time."

With regard to money, there are two equally healthy schools of thought.

    a) Expansion should be self financing.

    b) You should borrow at x % to earn x + y %.

Businesses in fast expanding market areas are generally easier to self finance as they generate a high cash flow.

In the slower growth markets, borrowing is more necessary your guideline here is that you must **know** within 1½ % what the nett profit expectation is going to be:— If you get a loser you're crying all the way to the bank.

Golden Facts: There is no such article as a stagnant business.

If your business isn't growing — It's dying.

* The Canal Age: Charles Hadfield; David and Charles series in Pan books.

11   Money Management

Golden Rule: Tend your money with care, like your own baby. Always know your financial position — precisely.

a) Background.

The raison d'etre of any business is to generate more profit than can be earned by placing it in a safe bank.

(And if you ever wanted proof that what you are doing is good for your fellow man, as well as yourself I commend to you St Luke ch. 19 v 11 — 27).

In other words if you currently earn £2,500 and have £10,000 to invest your profit opportunity must exceed £4,000 net, since you could (currently) earn £1,500 p.a. on your £10,000 investment.

In fact since you are putting your money and livelihood at risk, I'd recommend that unless you think that there's a fair chance of earning £6,000 in year one, and £8,000 in year two, you abandon the idea.

Incidentally, don't budget to make a loss, ever. The world and it's markets are so volatile that it is very difficult to predict the future (and with an incorrect prediction you can make some awfully bad judgements). Therefore it is very chancy to budget a loss this year, and a sufficiently attractive profit next year.

b) Money in Action.

The name of the game **is** money.

Whatever amount of money you have available to start your business, you need to generate a cash flow, — otherwise the cash will be travelling one way — out. In other words, it is essential that you start taking money — soon.

If you are manufacturing goods don't build up what an industrial giant would call "launch — stocks" — get the stuff out to your customers. It's more use to them than it is to you — and their money is your very life blood.

Don't forget that many companies are geared up to pay their bills at the end of the month following invoice — so get out as many goods as you can before the end of the month.

However you'll be needing as much money as you can get — quickly — so a good trick is to offer, say, a 5% settlement for payment within 10 days. If you do this you must be quick with your accounting — which is a good discipline.

However if you are running a retail business there is only one golden rule — NO TICK — AT ALL. One dishonest person can take away a whole week's profits, and no one's personal credit is as good as his money.

But let's distinguish between "tick" and credit facilities. There is absolutely no reason why you should not offer credit facilities as provided by the Finance Houses, you may even get a worthwhile commission out of it. You could also consider offering Barclaycard and Access facilities, but you must remember that in this case you must pay the credit card company a commission of between $2\frac{1}{2}\%$ — 5%.

When buying products for manufacturing or retail, use your money well. Don't overstock on super — duper — this — is — your — only — chance deals. Don't pay for goods until you have to, and take settlement discounts only if they are worthwhile to you.

Now above all, is the time to remember — The name of the game is money — no matter how much you enjoy the work, the product, or your working environment. Your own goal is the generation of more money than you put in. This is not only profit for you to spend on your pleasure — it is money to invest in growth to create more jobs and better jobs for your employees.

Golden Reminder: The target — is profit; measured ££££££.

No book which carries the odd quotation should be without some words of wisdom from Oscar Wilde and although this is not one of his best, it really does serve to reinforce the theme of this section.

"When I was young I used to think that money was the most important thing in life; now that I am old, I know it is."

Now money management is one area where expert help should be solicited all the way along the line — from before the time you begin your business, and every waking day you feel that it is necessary. Don't start looking for an accountant when you hit trouble, or to sort out your year-end accounts. We have talked briefly of cash-flow. A good accountant will explain what this means to you and your business. Below we give an example of cash-flow at work in a manufacturing business.

Cash flow can be described as a balance between the amount of money owed to you, and the amount you owe to other people. It affects the amount of business which you are able to transact.

If you have an input of £10,000, give 8 weeks credit to your debtors, and take 4 weeks credit from your creditors, your approximate effective cash availability is £10,000 ÷ 8 x 4 x 13 = £65,000 a year.

If you have an input of £10,000, limit your credit to 2 weeks, and take 8 weeks credit from your suppliers, your effective cash availability is £10,000 ÷ 2 x 8 x 13 = £520,000 a year.

Now these are rough and ready guidelines, but show the effect on your business that tight monetary and cash-flow controls can have. Taking this a stage further, we can show how cash-flow control can tighten your competitive edge.

You may argue that you are in a competitive industry where the length of credit you offer is a potent selling tool. The counter argument is that if reducing your credit lines from 8 weeks to 2 weeks allows you to produce (say) 3 times the amount of goods, then a lower nett %age profit will produce a higher total profit (without costing-in the additional benefits of the economies of scale and bulk-buying).

Example: You produce 1,000 units a year selling at £100 each, with a nett profit of £10 each. Total Profit £10,000.

By tightening credit lines, you produce 3,000 units a year selling at £95 each, with a nett profit of £5 each. Total Profit £15,000.

I hope it goes without saying that these facts are only true where it is the lack of finance which inhibits the growth of the business.

c) **Taxation.**

One of the unpleasant aspects of running your own business is the tax bills which you will have to face.

Wage and salary earners pay tax on a system designated Pay As You Earn (P.A.Y.E.) which supposedly works on the principle that if they take a drop at a time you won't feel the pain. (Though some would say it is more akin to Chinese Water Torture).

The self employed can find themselves confronted with many and varied taxes including income tax, and capital gains tax. The one thing that they all have in common is that they come suddenly, and can have a debilitating impact on any business which is unprepared for them. Again, a good accountant will help you structure your business to take advantage of current taxation legislation, and use that which is, after all, the taxman's money, to good purpose.

There are, however, two things which you should remember in favour of the tax authorities:

1. If you are earning money, you should be paying taxes, everyone else does! and the more tax you pay the more you must be earning. (which, you will remember, is our goal in life).

2. Everyone but your favoured group pays their tax weekly or monthly as it is due. As a self-employed person for the first

year at least, you pay over a year in arrears, and have use of money to which morally, if not legally, you can hardly be said to be entitled.

Golden Advice: Don't try to cheat the taxman. It is illegal, it is immoral, and if that is not bad enough, if your staff see you doing it, they'll adopt the attitude that if you cheat, they can too. Only the person cheated will be YOU.

12 Keeping Down Overheads.

Golden Rule: Keep a firm grip on the purse strings.

Now here's a place where you can score over the big companies.

Delegate everything you like, but make sure you keep a tight hold on the purse strings — and remember, it's your money.

In big business, managers employ a technique called budgetary control.

i.e. They budget to sell £x million at a profit level of £y million, to enable them to do this they are allowed to spend £z thousand, and believe me, they'll spend it. (The more money they control, the bigger their job, their scope of authority — which is really why they are there — and perhaps the bigger their salary).

Your problem is not to find ways to spend your budget.

It is to ask questions.

Like: Will it save someone time?

> If he isn't fully employed do we need to save his time just now?

> Will we learn more? — and if we learn more will we earn more?

> In other words — from this cash output will there be a greater cash input and if so — when, and how big will it be?

If anyone were able to survey how much money is **wasted** in big companies or even medium sized companies a scandal would emerge that would make Watergate look like stealing cakes at Noddy's Tea party.

Allow me to show you ten easy ways to waste money.

1) Give everyone an office graded by size and quality of furnishings in order of supposed importance.
2) Distribute company cars like maundy money.

3) Have the head office in the parent companies premises, and the actual business more than 3 miles away.
4) Have a prestige anything — office block, product or sports club.
5) Prepare impressive annual reports.
6) Publish house magazines.
7) Spend money on promoting "a corporate image."
8) Employ people as "assistants to".
9) Have liason men or co-ordinators.
10) How's your chauffeur?

One of the biggest ways to lose money in any business is **theft.** A friend of mine who owns two chains of shops, one a first rate supermarket chain, the other a discount clothing chain tells me that he could earn a very respectable living advising any group of 50 shops or more on security, and just taking 1% of anything he saves them on stock shrinkage over the previous year. That's how big the problem is. It would be foolish of me to attempt to cover the subject within these pages.

Just be alive to the problem. And if you find staff thieving — sack'em and customers pinching — hand them over to the police. (It's less vindictive and costly than personal prosecution).

Another friend of mine had his own peculiar method of dealing with the one defaulter he came across.

Some eight months after he had received a "bounced" cheque from this customer he met him in the street, he picked him up and hung the man by his jacket on some railings until he went to summon the police.

The papers got hold of this and published it, and he's not had a single "bounced" cheque since.

Golden Advice: Keep asking dem questions.

13 Honesty is Not the Best Policy.

Golden Rule: Honesty is not the best policy — it is the only policy.

My old grandmother used to say "be sure your sins will find you out." She used to say lots of other things too — but this one is really worth remembering. If you are dishonest, even slightly dishonest, just once, the news will spread like wildfire.

If you are honest, completely and scrupulously honest nobody will mention it — but you should at least sleep soundly at night.

An old saying, as true now as it was a hundred years ago: "Prefer a loss to a dishonest gain; the one brings pain at the moment, the other for all time."

Remember too that if you begin to show signs of success the knockers will get to work trying to shatter your image, and more important, your business.

The nicest thing a knocker will say about you is that you are lucky (never mind about the risks you've taken, the hours of sweat and toil you've put in). Just make sure that the knockers have nothing to really get their teeth into.

The other day I was talking to a non-business man who told me "If I was to go into business I'd form a limited company so that I wouldn't be in for much if it went sour." (Limited is short for limited liability where the liability of the owner is limited to a certain sum of money).

Three points here.

Firstly it is unlikely that such a company would be granted credit without the personal guarantee and security of the major shareholder.

Secondly if the company is moderately successful a tax disadvantage could accrue.

Thirdly if you're so worried about the possible viability don't start the business in the first place.

Golden Advice: Keep your personal, homelife, record sheet clean.

More **Golden Advice**: Become limited only on the advice of a professional accountant.

14 Advertising and Sales Promotion.

Golden Rule: Measure the effect of every £ spent.

Like all specialist tasks here is a subject best left to experts. But do remember that nobody knows your business and it's objectives like you do. So if you decide to appoint an advertising agency, do be sure you give it the fullest possible brief.

If you are starting a small business, pick a small agency where your billing (expenditure) might count, and ensure that initially your problem is inspected by a senior account handler.

If the agency questions all aspects of your business, including product range, who is going to buy it and how and where you are going to sell it, you will probably get reasonably good advertising. If they don't ask these questions you will probably get a pretty picture and a few bad words.

Let the agency know you want to measure every £ spent, and ensure that you know how much they will charge you, in advance, at every step of every job.

Measuring the effect of advertising is very difficult. There is a legend in the advertising industry (and try as I might I cannot locate the source) that "Half the money I spend on advertising is wasted — the question is — which half?."

However what you can do is make a rough assessment to see whether your advertising is working for you — or even against you.

These are three major methods of influencing people's thinking towards your product or your shop,

a) **Public relations,** through local media (newspapers and radio).

Something interesting happens to your products, or company (it can be contrived by yourself — such as paying a personality to visit your factory), you advise the press and local radio in advance, or following the event. If they consider the item newsworthy, or interesting (good copy) you may get some useful coverage.

There are obvious disadvantages to this method of promotion (lack of control, of both message and timing) — but it does have one major advantage which you can't really beat, of being free.

b) **Sales promotions.**

These are usually of short term duration and number some of the following devices.

10% off all stock, this week only (good if you have too much stock). 20% off certain items (good if you have stock balance problems).

Free daffodil, holiday to daffodil fields, pair of binoculars, polaroid camera, competition to win a car, Caribbean holiday etc. etc.

Sales promotions are generally a short term tactic designed to achieve a certain purpose, and are not considered as a method retaining customers loyalty. There is however one exception to this, which is the cigarette coupon, or gift stamp type promotion.

c) **Media advertising** — on radio, television, or in the newspapers.

This gives you publicity Where you want it.

When you want it.

In the form that you want it.

But it does cost money, and people may not believe it.

Golden Advice: Never believe your own publicity.

It's there for others to believe, your job is not only to match up to it, but to exceed it.

So set your publicity target high, then make sure that you achieve your target in your performance.

If you feel that you should know more about advertising in order to be a better businessman, may I suggest you read "Advertising for the Advertiser — A Clients Guide" by Eric Webster, 1969. Published by John Murray, 50, Albemarle St., London WIX 4BD. with which, I promise, you will not be bored.

15 How to Start Selling.

Golden Rule: Roly poly — ever so slowly.
Roly poly — ever so fast. (childrens game-anon).

The first few weeks of your business, be it retailing or manufacturing, you must find your feet without the great mass of people seeing you making your mistakes, but as soon as you are ready, go like mad!

My mistake was to mass advertise too soon, before I had sufficient stock and knowledge to back the advertising — so we had hundreds of people coming to buy next-to-nothing.

The mistake was created by longer-than-normal local advertising lead times, so that we had to book space three weeks in advance. And in that three weeks we had an awful number of setbacks. The mistake cost £450 and a lot of lost goodwill.

Many years ago I worked for a successful company who were about to launch a new and highly technical product — of a type which we had not made before. The production cycle on all new products followed the pattern below.

Research and Development	Hand made finished samples for test and transit	Preproduction run	Iron out bugs	Mass market

The preproduction run, on a special production line would indicate any manufacturing problems, allow us to send finished samples to our overseas agents for their comments and permit us to evaluate the product packaging. The iron out bugs period being flexible from three weeks to three months according to the problems which we found.

However we hit many snags on the run up to the product and so it slipped farther and farther behind schedule and we built up quite a backlog of unfinished goods stocks — so much so that it was affecting our capacity to buy parts for our ongoing line of products.

A decision was taken to miss out the preproduction run, iron out the bugs during production, and plunge in with both feet. What a disaster. The advertising was booked against a production forecast, which it was not possible to achieve (but who was to know it?). In fact we never achieved a 50% level of production although the product had a three year life cycle — therefore we never managed to satisfy the demand the advertising created, or recoup the cost of the initial advertising, because the production time was so slow the product was wrongly costed, and we had to more than double the labour content cost.

Furthermore for the first six months of it's life cycle the product suffered an above average failure rate due to supplier deficiencies in components. (Which would undoubtedly have been spotted in a preproduction run). And so it goes on. Please heed the warning. Fortunately we were able to carry on with our other product line, which bolstered up this product until it became self sufficient after fourteen months of it's life.

(Both these instances go to show that you can be successful after making such mistakes — nil desperandum).

Golden Advice: Remain calm.

16 Customers: How to Find Them. (Promotion)

Golden Rule: Never miss an opportunity of making a sale — anywhere (even the local pub — at the risk of becoming a bore).

Customers are easy to find — there are over 50 million of them in the U.K. Your objective is to locate your **Prime** market, the one which your message will reach most effectively.

If you have a corner shop your prime market is probably within an 80 yard radius, so you can find your customers by knocking on peoples doors, standing outside factory gates (or if you prefer to put it into advertising terms — leaflets through the door, leaflets into the factory, and perhaps a billboard hoarding outside). Your best advertisement is undoubtably your shop (visually) and the service you offer.

If you are a league football team your prime market is the locality, unless you are in the superstar class when you don't need to worry about finding your customers — they'll find you.

You could find customers in your locality by advertising in the local press — or at other football grounds, or in the Sunday league publication.

If you are selling expensive motor cars, publications like Autocar and Motor will locate the prime market. So will the Motor Show, as possibly will race meetings, hill climbs, and go-cart racing.

If your prime market is the well heeled countryman try the Tattersalls enclosure at your local racecourse.

The list is endless. All you need to know is:

Who are the prime market.

Then ask the question, how can I most effectively communicate with this group of people.

Do remember that your communication need not be "flash" to be effective.

One retailer (6 branches) of quality Hi Fi consumer durables has tried all the sophisticated methods to drum up business. — Press releases, letters to the papers — Advertising in local press — In national special interest magazines — In national press (mail order) — Advertising on T.V. — Late night openings — Mass demonstrations — Sale weeks in quiet periods.

His single most effective method of finding extra customers involves giving away a double page price list with special "buy now" incentive (£5 voucher off £100 goods, an extra year's free service — this month only) — The leaflet is given away **outside** an exhibition which promotes the products which he sells.

No extra staff are employed — the idea is simplicity itself— and **the big companies are not prepared to lower themselves to this kind of promotion.**

In fact the only other retail company giving away leaflets in this way at this exhibition are also very successful, although with no special offers — just a first class service — and this is the only method of advertising they employ!!

If you are a manufacturer looking for customers, either industrial users or retail / wholesale outlets, you will no doubt find that a "direct mail company" will be able to provide you with a list to whom they will mail out advertising material on your behalf.

Our Golden Advice: Is to buy a good list, but do not adopt a mail-shot canvass in the first instance, this will be the first contact between you and your new potential customer. If you blow it, it could be the kiss of death.

You should use one of the three methods of approach as suits your operation best.

    a) Cold Canvass. You visit the company and request to see
       buyer — start from scratch.

b) Telephone Canvass. You ring the buyer and sound out his interest, having given him the background to your story. You arrange an interview if it would appear he may be interested.

c) Letter canvass to a named person. You write a letter to a high-up in the company (it's amazing how people respond to letters passed down to them, rather than one passed up or across).

The content of the letter gives a background and reason why the company would benefit from a discussion and you suggest that you will ring to arrange an appointment on such and such a date.

If your proposition is unlikely to be acceptable you will no doubt receive a letter in advance of the date.

The benefits of each of the above methods are outlined below;

Advantages.	Disadvantages.
a) High call rate, No missed opportunities, Good for where wide distribution required	Expensive. High wastage rate.
b) The inbetween route; major advantage is speed.	Major disadvantage is lack of "opportunity to see" either product, person, or written material.
c) Good for creating impression possible "inertia" sell (chairman writes on letter to buyer "this looks like a good idea Joe" — even if buyer thinks it's rubbish).	People might not fully read or understand.
Time saving — all calls by appointment — all likely conversions.	Might say no to this before being exposed to persuasive tongue.

Do you remember our section "A place for everything?"

As a manufacturer it may be no bad thing to have your orders in the bag before you start producing.

The major disadvantage is that you will give your competitors advance warning of your intentions, which will allow them to react more quickly than they might otherwise have done.

The advantage is that you have your sales forecast (and therefore your production forecast) written for you by your customers.

17 Customers, How to Keep Them.

Golden Rule: Customers are King. Treat them regally.

In a word what you must give to your customers is "service." If you serve them well, they will reciprocate in the time honoured manner with orders, or business.

Only **you** know the type of service your customer will require and if you don't know, or aren't too sure, don't be afraid of asking.

The wrong kind of service is worse than no service at all, for not only does your customer not want it, he will feel that you do not fully understand his problems, and that you have not got close enough to him and his business or requirements.

If you have a retail business, the service you can offer can be based around opening hours, display and demonstration, instant availability, delivery and installation service, guarantee repair service, out of guarantee returns, credit terms, extra guarantees, free home trials, loan of goods while his are being serviced.

An example of the wrong kind of service, could be after selling a colour t.v. to a colour t.v. engineer, offering free replacement set should his go wrong. He'd be more likely to thank you for a circuit diagram and instant spare parts after he had diagnosed the fault, and if you come up with the goods he'd be likely to buy his next set from you too (and his washer and fridge).

Customer loyalty is however much more essential to a manufacturing business.

Services common to both retail and manufacturing include opening hours (accessability), customer education, (display), availability on request, quick turn-round on faulty units, (transit damage replacements), credit terms, service stock.

Service exclusive to manufacturing for industry include stock holding for customer, working together with engineers, product designers in early stages of product, designing one-offs to handle a particular job.

43

As an example of working closely with a customer, knowing his problems, and offering a service which wins the sale, I quote to you the glue salesman to the loudspeaker factory. Not particularly exciting stuff, but most money making isn't.

The loudspeaker company makes very good loudspeakers, so good that the glue must not just stick metal to cloth, cloth to paper, paper to non woven fabric to metal. It must do so with a certain amount of elasticity so that the characteristics of cloth, paper and non woven fabrics are not affected.

The glue salesman does not say number 87a will do this — or offer a list of glues for sticking metal to cloth etc..

He takes away the component parts to his laboratory and returns 2-3 weeks later with samples of glues appropriate (for sticking purposes). The loudspeaker engineers then test the glues for elasticity and the end result in terms of standard of performance and if they are able to they specify one or more of these off-the-shelf samples. Otherwise they may brief the glue company to produce a special glue.

Because of this special service, the glue company gets the order, the functions of price, credit, availability are also important, but they play second fiddle to a service in this instance.

Obviously if they cannot back up this service with a high standard of product or they fail to deliver and cause the cardinal sin of allowing the production line to stop, the glue people will be out on their ears or come unstuck!!

Golden Advice: If you can't do it, or aren't too sure, don't promise it. Only make realistic promises.

18 Buying.

But to sell well, first you need to buy well. And to buy well you must follow the

Golden Rule: Always have a second source of supply for every item in your range.

Don't mind how good a price / delivery you get from your first source. One day he'll let you down. So you either do without (and can you do without it if you're in manufacturing?) or you turn the second source on strong.

No scurrying round in a panic for your second source.

I once worked in an industry where many manufacturers bought a component from one source. A very reliable highly organised source, whose service was so impeccable that many highly professional giants of industry didn't bother to second source the component. Then one night disaster fell. The factory burned down. The tap was turned off overnight.

Highly paid purchasing executives with egg on their faces jetted off all over the world in search of a now scarce resource. It would be funny if it wasn't so tragic. Please don't let it happen to you.

Furthermore if you second source everything, you'll be first in line for news of special deals, or product improvements from the eager beaver trying to tie up your business.

And while we're on the subject of eager beavers, never ever refuse to see a company sales representative unless you are really pressed for time (in which case can you fix to see him later).

Sales representatives offer you opportunities, by all means reject them if they don't suit you, but don't let them pass you by, by failing to inspect them.

During my days as a retailer my biggest competitor did me a huge favour, by failing to see a representative (because he "did not deal with that company"), I was left with a unique Christmas line which earned me an extra £200. Not a lot of money perhaps, but more useful in my pocket than my competitors. My competitor saved himself five minutes, I invested my five minutes. Now it doesn't always work like that, but providing you keep a firm grip on your objectives, you can generally make every conversation work for you. Your objective might be to find out what a competitor is doing / buying, what successful promotional methods other people have used. You might be wanting to make a point that you are prepared to buy if you can have extra credit / terms.

But whatever you do, don't chinwag. Don't gossip (listen if you must) and don't waste your time on non essential chat.

If you must indulge in gossip with salesman, do it out of hours at your own expense (that way you'll only do it if it's really worth it — and you won't be guilty of wasting valuable working time).

One fact that I learnt during my early days was that many suppliers are inefficient and make quite elementary mistakes, and I seemed to be burdened with that horror "double delivery." Two I sent back, and then I called a company to ask them to take away a double delivery but their sales manager said, (not verbatim) "Look it's an honest mistake, but to come and uplift it will cost us a lot of money and effort. If you keep the second delivery we'll give you an extra three months credit on the second lot and an extra 2½% discount on both lots as an inconvenience fee. It's our way of saying we're sorry and in fact it's costing us very little."

Fortunately it was a fast moving line so I readily agreed. I also made the offer to other people making the same mistake later.

We include a feature later on covering "negotiation," don't forget you can negotiate on all sorts of aspects of your business.

Finally on the subject of buying, never get delusions of grandeur. Buy at the best economic terms, but never overbuy to impress. There are too many stories around about people losing their liquidity through over buying and having to sell out for coppers. If they have this problem I hope it's because they misestimated the market — not because someone got too big for his boots and put his mouth where his money wasn't, which brings us on to another piece of advice.

Golden Advice: Keep emotion out of all your business decisions.

19 Business Confidence.

Golden Rule: Build confidence.

There's a lot of talk today from football managers about their players confidence in their abilities. These managers spend a substantial part of their time just building the players' confidence, in themselves as individuals and as a team.

The same is true of your business.

Your employees must be confident of the future and quality of their business. I used to work for a firm where a sign of an employees success was that he managed to avoid the Friday afternoon chop in his bosses office. (In the less than two years that I was there the staff dropped from over 400 to under 200).

The problem had been created by a government who decided to move our product from being untaxed to carry a 50% purchase tax rate — overnight.

However it was our problem to solve, and although we managed to retain our turnover, and our profits, just about everyone lost confidence in his ability to make business grow, the atmosphere bred too many "dismal jimmies". It's often good to have one or two of these prophets of doom around — if only for everyone else to take the mickey. But when everyone is singing the same song it could finish up being a dirge.

Employees confidence will also lead to customer confidence. No customer will buy a fridge or a machine tool from a company he is not confident will be around to service it.

A friend of mine fortuitously cancelled his continental holiday with a now defunct travel company, because of a conversation between two clerks in a travel agency indicating lack of confidence in the travel trade as a whole in early 1974.

The conversation, repeated in many agencies across the country, may have not only helped in the downfall of that travel company, but also in the down turn of trade in general.

Had these two persons not exposed their lack of confidence on this particular occasion there would certainly have been a further £400 in the coffers.

So all the time you should be working to build confidence. And when you've got confidence you'll find that (again to use a term oft quoted by football managers) you will make your own luck.

You'll find people wanting to back you, lend you money, work for you, and buy from you. What else could you ask for?

Golden Advice: Build confidence, — but do remember our policy of honesty — and statement made by Robert Louis Stevenson — The Cruellest lies are often told in silence.

20 How to build up a Run Down Business

Golden Rule: Find out what is keeping buyers away from the door and be ruthless with it.

Essentially you can successfully build up a run-down business by following the advice given in this book.

There are however certain extra problems which you may face as a result of getting into something which is alive, if not kicking.

We will assume that the reason that the business is run down, is because it has insufficient customers, or insufficient profits from sufficient customers.

You must, when moving into a run-down business ensure that you have sufficient capital to take you through lean times before you begin to bring home the bacon. This is because any changes you make, are likely to lose you some of the existing customers before you begin to acquire new customers.

Perhaps a couple of working examples will help to paint a more accurate picture.

The corner shop which Mr. and Mrs. Smith have run for 8 years has had a steadily declining trade; in order to increase trade they have given "tick." This has strapped them for cash, so that they have found it hard to pay their bills. Therefore they have reduced their stockholding and choice, so they get less customers.

You move in, and determine that customers must have more choice — giving them more choice will increase your throughput and therefore provide you with quantity discounts which you will use to modernise, advertise or pass on in price reductions. But to give the choice, you need to restrict "tick" to increase cash flow. Some people will be unhappy to trade with you, therefore you will lose an amount of custom.

On a larger scale, a major American manufacturer of processed foods, had, due to successively bad marketing policies arrived at the position where, although it had sufficient customers, and kept the plant working at satisfactory capacities, profits were extremely low. The accounts of the company were audited quarterly, and the grocery trade knew this — so they refused to buy in the first two months of the quarter, 80% of the sales coming in the last 3 weeks of the last month. Because less than 20% of capacity had been sold in the first 2 months, huge bonuses were offered in the third to encourage the trade to stock-in. This situation, which had not, of course, come about overnight, continued to grow, through a succession of marketing managers, until one day a bright young thing arrived in that exalted position and determined that he had moved into a run down business.

He therefore went to the managing director and promised him one disastrous period, followed by one almost as bad, followed by a period which would put the business back on it's feet on a higher profitability platform than ever before. He was able to promise this because he had a quality product with a high consumer franchise.

At the end of the first period the trade, although they had been warned that all "deals" were off were surprised when no "deals" were forthcoming. But they knew, or thought they knew, what would happen at the end of the next accounting period. (All the same they began to buy the product in small amounts). When again no deals were offered, they were amazed. And because of the pressure of consumer demand they were obliged to stock at non bonus terms in large quantities once more.

The marketing manager was able to honour his promise to the managing director, and both went on to further glorious successes. But that decision took a tremendous amount of guts. Guts from the marketing manager, who put his job on the line 9 months on, and even more guts from the managing director, who borrowed money to keep his production lines going and pay his staff during a period when only 25% of his turnover was coming in the regular way.

Your decision in building up a run-down business will be smaller — but when it's your own money and your own trade that you are cutting back the decision requires so much more guts.

The lesson to be learned here, is that when you buy a run-down business you should pay no heed to past earnings or future potential in the purchase price.

Consider whether you would now be better starting from scratch — or if you decide to buy, the sales price must take into account a projected drop in volume early on in the life of the business.

One couple I know had a great deal of success in building up run-down newsagencies. Their policy was a very simple one.

Firstly they totally cleared the shop of slow moving stock. They brightened up the shop with a lick of paint, restocked it with merchandise they knew would sell, standardised the daily opening hours, (7-7 including Sundays) kept a full range of all the newspapers, magazines etc., smiled at everyone who came in and employed pleasant, hardworking staff.

Although the turnover never dropped, in each shop they always throw away a lot of newspapers, particularly in the first instance.

The charm of the operation was that they never intended to build a business for their own use,. but to resell at a profit.

I met them in 1962 when they had been successful four times already and were on their fifth venture, there is no reason why they should not be still doing it.

The mathematics can be quite astonishing.

		Annual Nett Make £
June 1962	Take over shop for £4,000 net profit £1,000	500
June 1963	Increase earnings to £1,600	1,600
June 1964	Increase earnings to £2,200	2,200
June 1965	Sell shop for £8,800 (nett profit rate £2,200)	
June 1965	Buy larger shop for £8,800 (nett profit rate £2,000)	2,100
June 1966	Increase earnings to £3,000	3,000
June 1967	Increase earnings to £3,500	3,500
June 1968	Sell shop for £14,000 (net profit rate £3,300)	
June 1968	Buy larger shop for £13,000 (nett profit rate £3,250);	3,375
June 1969	Increase earnings to £4,000	4,000
June 1970	Increase earnings to £4,800 Value of bus. £19,200	4,800

(All buying and selling is done at Four Times earnings).

The figures are simply to show that mathematically it is possible to increase the value of your original investment by a large amount. These figures may be net of inflation, and therefore demonstrate real growth.

Golden Advice: Consider very carefully whether to purchase a run-down business. You may do better to start up a similar venture from scratch, next door, in the next street, or in the next town.

21 Special Skills —
a) How to Use Them

Golden Rule: Harness the skills available to you, and use them with the utmost efficiency.

We have already talked about the use of outsiders in your business, Accountants, Solicitors, Advertising Agency.

But what about the people within?

Even if it is only yourself and your wife each of you has your own skill.

Make sure that each of you uses his skill to the full.

If you have a small shop, and your wife is pleasant and persuasive let her do the bulk of the selling — if you drive a hard bargain and have a head for figures you should do the buying, (but don't forget to ask her what she can sell).

On a bigger scale you may find that whilst you have overall charge of the company you have a particular talent for picking the right workers. — Use it (in conjunction with your colleagues). But if you employ a man to be Personnel Manager he should have this skill, so make sure he uses it (one of the most Quoted business / advertising phrases — It's no good buying a dog and barking yourself).

Please remember when you grow so big that you need managers and supervisors etc. that the best salesmen or foremen do not necessarily make the best sales managers or works managers. Managerial positions require different skills.

A friend of mine earns £4,000 as a sales manager of a successful company. His best salesman earns almost £5,000.

His best salesman will probably never earn much more than £5,000 — as this is the limit of his sales ability, and he does not command the respect of his fellow salesmen (except for his sales technique).

My friend who, as well as being a talented salesman is a brilliant man manager will go on to bigger and better things. My friend would not be human if he did not envy his best salesman from time to time — but he is professional enough to realise that his best salesman is a major contributory factor in his own success story.

Let's have a look at another successful business manager turned failure — we shall have to call him manager A.

His skills were undoubtably the selling and administration aspects of a in a medium sized retail chain. He also did the buying, but not so well. The company brought in a manager (B) at manager A level, as a buyer / administrator to help ease the burden on manager A who would be free to concentrate on selling. Manager A thought that this would seem to the trade that he was junior to manager B — and furthermore he enjoyed many perks which buyers are given.

He therefore persuaded his boss that the split should not be buying / selling, but that both A and B should do similar jobs but across different product ranges.

B at once demonstrated that not only was he a brilliant buyer — but his administration and selling techniques were every bit as good as A's.

Result: A was sacked. B was promoted slightly and given two assistants to help him do his job.

Perhaps A will realise that his failure is not that he bought badly, but that he did not use his special skills to good effect.

Buying brings us to a part of business which can make or lose you money, overnight, than any other.

21 Special Skills
b) The art of negotiation.

And it really is an art, because it cannot be taught, only learnt by experience, practice, and "gut — feel."

But even with art there are a few rules to follow. I assume incidentally that you are either buying or selling a business, a major capital item, or a large supply of goods.

1) Determine the value of the object of the negotiation to you as a buyer or seller. If the value to you may differ from its real value and you are unable to assess its real value, get an expert to value it for you. (Better still, if it's really valuable get two).

2) Having determined the value, set yourself very firmly a maximum buying price or minimum selling price, above or below which you will not go.

3) If the other person is reticent, make the first bid or offer with confidence.

4) If selling, ask for a figure above what you expect to achieve, if buying somewhat below. One cannot fix a % age — this is where experience of the product, the deal and the other party come in (you must be able to justify the figure asked — of course).

5) Do not be afraid that the other party will laugh at you. He may, but it really is a pathetic ploy. Say something like, "I can't understand why you are laughing — after all you were unable to make me an offer — I think my deal is worth £3,000 because — — — — — —" you will then retain the upper hand and can ask at the end. "Can I assume that you will be able to meet the asking price?"

Then wait for his answer. Don't speak. Anything you say after this juncture must be a concession — so seal them lips.

Eventually one of two things will happen.

    a) You will come to an agreement within both your and the other parties selling / buying price spectrum and conclude a deal.

    b) This is not possible due to incompatibility or lack of capital or something.

        In this case you can discuss terms and methods of payments.

        Or you can appoint a negotiator (not an arbitrator) who will discuss the matter with each of you privately and possibly work out a mutually satisfactory deal.

A negotiator in the above case would probably be used because either or both of the parties have secrets which they wish to keep from each other, yet which have a bearing on the negotiation.

Golden Advice: i) If you can't negotiate for yourself you should appoint someone to act on your behalf. I have a feeling, which I cannot quantify, that there are very few good negotiators about — so un' cc you know someone with a good track record I would strongly recommend you to try and tackle this one yourself.

ii) If you are buying **anything** substantial **always** try to negotiate a better price.

22 Start Working.

Golden Rule: All work and no play makes Jack a rich boy.

Well it's up to you. I haven't told you **all** I know — I've been working now in businesses of some sort or another, my own and other people's for fifteen years — but you've enough in this book to give you the foundation for a very successful business of your own.

Use the rules and advice as you think fit.

Don't throw the book away, or lend it to anyone else though — (not just because I want to sell more copies).

Keep it as a staff to lean on, or a friend to help you when you come to a problem you haven't faced before. Read it again every three or four months to remind you of some of the rules, and the stories of other people.

All the stories in the book are true, or told to me as true, anonymity has been observed for very obvious reasons.

If you have a story you'd like to tell, or a problem, write to me at the publishers, and I guarantee you an answer if your letter asks for one. (Though the reply may be delayed as I spend a lot of time away from home).

To help you further we've included after this piece a short chapter on when to sell a business, and a summary of the golden rules and advice. And to really make things simple a set of golden checklists, containing some of the information in the book, and some commonsense items which might get lost in your overwhelming enthusiasm.

Remember what you are doing or are about to do is very hard work — but if you do it right (and I've deliberately not mentioned the word before — PROFESSIONALLY) — you will make some money, have some fun, and eventually gain the respect of many of the people you currently admire.

Good Luck.

23 When to Sell a Business.

By the time you need any advice on this subject you will have already acquired a large amount of experience yourself. You may be well aware of the times when you should sell, or dispose of a business.

Summarised.

1) When you are making a loss and can see no way out.
2) When you are bored, unhappy or not achieving job satisfaction (even if you are very successful — you may not be happy — but what about considering expansion?)
3) When somebody asks you to sell to them (however they dress it up, they want your business and will undoubtedly be prepared to offer you more than its real worth).
4) When you have achieved a certain goal, and wish to acquire capital to chase some other goal.
5) Whenever you can get two or more persons really interested in the purchase of your business — to such an extent that they compete to buy — (supply and demand says that when there's only one to buy and two people want it then the one selling wins).

There are however outside forces at work which can substantially alter the value of your business over which you have no control. These are generally of a long term nature, and they do leave you with certain options.

At the end of a generally depressed business period (nationally) you wish to sell — but bright times are coming.

If you sell you will not get what the business is really worth, but you will be free to do what you want. If you retain the business you will begin to earn much more money, and the business will substantially increase in value.

But when the time of plenty is seen to come to an end your business will be worth less than it was 6 months previously; Therefore you won't get as much for it as you would have done and you may have built up a price in your imagination below which you are not prepared to go.

Somewhere there is the happy medium which suits you and a buyer — in terms of timing, price and payment terms.

It's rather like the stock market — where the number of people who buy shares at the bottom and sell at the top can be counted on the fingers of one foot.

Other factors which may affect the value of your business, are the effects of competition, population movements, consumer requirements and the time of year. (you'll get a lot more for a toyshop in November than in February, or a boarding house in March rather than October).

It really points to you being just as professional in the sale of your business as you are in the running of it.

Think about this: It really is rather silly spending a lot of time and risking all your money building up a business, if you do not fully capitalise on it when you sell it.

Author's P.S.

I am not, have never been, and probably never will be the owner of a Wellington Boot Supermarket in Lower King St. Manchester.

I have little knowledge of Manchester, and even less of wellington boot marketing.

I am also absolutely certain that any such venture would be the most likely failure since the South Sea Bubble.

Please don't use it, as an idea, to prove me right or wrong.

Appendix I

SUMMARY OF GOLDEN RULES.

1) Know your subject.
2) Take advantage of the opportunities as they arise.
3) If you are not prepared for total committal, do not commit yourself at all.
4) Pick associates whose specialty will help you and your problems.
5) Have a plan and monitor your progress against it as often as you can.
6) a. Obtain property you can equally easily dispose of.
   b. Select the least expensive accommodation that will do the job adequately.
7) When selecting staff, be very very careful.
8) Don't let the business run you.
9) If you want to delegate work, you must delegate most of the responsibility that goes with it.
10) Expand with caution.
11) Tend your money with care, like your own baby. Always know your financial position, precisely.
12) Keep a grip on the purse strings.
13) Honesty is not the **best** policy. It's the only policy.
14) Measure the effect of every £ spent on advertising.
15) Roly poly — ever so slowly
    Roly poly — ever so fast.
16) Never miss an opportunity of making a sale.
17) Customers are king. Treat them regally.
18) Always have a second source of supply for every item in your range.
19) Build confidence.
20) Find out what is keeping buyers away from the door and be ruthless with it.
21) Harness the skills available to you, and use them with the utmost efficiency.
22) All work and no play makes Jack a rich boy.

Appendix II

SUMMARY OF GOLDEN ADVICE, FACTS, WARNINGS.

1) Beware of setting up in price competition with a business with fat profits or easily prunable overheads.
2) If you can see ahead of you, events which could radically affect the course of your business, prepare contingency plans, before the pressure is on.
3) Persistance is it's own reward (but only if the graph is on an upward trend).
4) Weigh advice very carefully.
5) If you drift off plan and are unsuccessful don't be afraid to quit. No use being a damn fool about it.
6) Never be afraid to employ a specialist, particularly in the field of real estate.
7) Those staff who you value highly — overpay.
8) Make sure you can leave your business anytime you like for two weeks holiday.
9) If you've picked the wrong person as an employee, don't compound the error — fire the offender.
10) If your business isn't growing — It's dying.
11) a. The target is profit, measured £££££.
    b. Don't try to cheat the tax-man.
12) Don't spend more than a couple of pounds without asking WHY?
13) a. Keep your personal life clean.
    b. Become limited only on the advice of a professional accountant.
14) Set you publicity target high, then make sure you reach it in your performance.
15) Remain calm.
16) Find your prime market by buying the information from a mailing house (if you have to).
17) Only make realistic promises.
18) Keep emotion out of **all** your business decisions.
19) Build confidence — but not false confidence.

20) Consider — should I buy a run down business — or start up a new one?
21) a. If you can't negotiate — get someone who can act for you.
b. If you are buying anything substantial, always try to negotiate a better price.
22) Keep this book by you. Read it again and again.

Appendix III

GOLDEN CHECKLISTS — FOR A GOLDEN FUTURE.

How to use the checklists

1) First, read and fully understand all the "book" section of this material.

   Without this understanding, these checklists are empty shells.

2) Then read and answer, on a separate sheet, all the questions on the checklist.

3) Make any corrections to your plans you feel are necessary.

4) Keep the answers to your checklist, and note the date of your answers.

5) Refer to the checklist every three months or so and again write your answers down. Compare your answers against previous answers, and against the performance of your business (moving totals).

6) Has any action you have taken had a dramatic effect on the performance of your business?

7) Keep referring to the checklists — they are your self discipline and your tutor.

CHECKLIST NUMBER 1

a) What is / was your subject?
b) What will your business be / is your business?
c) Do a and b tie in?
   If not can you be **really** sure what you are doing?
   If no — go away and think about it.
d) Do you know the competition?
   All of it?
   What it is doing?
   What it / they may do when you begin to foul up their nests?
e) Are you missing any better opportunities by following this course?
   Are you sure they aren't better?
f) Are you flexible enough to be able to change course slightly — but instantly?
g) What will you do if this business fails?

CHECKLIST NUMBER 2

a) Give three good reasons for starting your business.
b) Analyse them.
   Are they **good** reasons?
c) Have you got what it takes?
   (i)   Will you work 18 hours a day 7 days a week?
   (ii) Have you the temperament and persistance to bounce back after crushing set backs?
   (iii) Can you do what you are expected to do now — with ease?
   (iv) Have you got guts?
   (v)   And a strong sense of humour?
         and if you're married.
   (vi) Will your spouse back you 100%.
d) Are you prepared to accept a cut in your standard of living for an indeterminate period?

CHECKLIST NUMBER 3

a) Have you spoken to;

A Bank Manager.
A Business Transfer Agent.
A Accountant.
A Solicitor.
A Window Cleaner.
A Potential Customer.
Another Local Trader.
A Competitor.
A Man-in the street.
An Advertising Man.
Another Potential Customer.
About Business and your Business.

This week

Why not?
Aren't you interested in your business or people?

b) O.K. We'll let you off with 7 out of 11 weekly if your 7 include the potential customers, and you talk to all 11 each month.

c) Have you aired a problem with a personal friend recently?

CHECKLIST NUMBER 4

a) Have you done a business plan?
b) What is the sales forecast?
c) What is the gross profit?
d) What is the overhead forecast?
e) What is the net profit?
f) Is this an optimistic forecast?
g) Is it really all worth it?

Write down the answer why? then turn the page.

If your answer doesn't say money, forget the idea and give the book to someone else.

If however you have already started your own business read on.

h) How are you matching up to your forecast?

 i) Are your overheads too high?

ii) If sales aren't correspondingly high — how will you cut them?

iii) Are the sales up to prediction — if not how will you stimulate more?

iv) Are you roaring ahead on sales and profits? — if so how will you increase your staff to cope.

 i) Can you see any long term trends that you should be trying to head-off — or conversely improve upon — at this early stage.

CHECKLIST NUMBER 5

a) Have you got the premises?
b) Is it big enough
   i) But not too big if you shoot 20% under plan?
   ii) Or too small if you shoot 20% over plan
c) Will it allow you the growth pattern in your plan?
d) How about the cost / size ratio?
   i) Are you going to use it all — you pay rent and rates on every inch.
e) Can you dispose of it easily?
   i) How do you know — have you tried?
f) How much will it cost you in initial and annual maintenance costs
   i) Have you made a complete allowance for this in your plan?
g) Will customers / workers be available?
   i) In sufficient quantities?
   ii) Always?
h) How's your voice these days? Still using it?

CHECKLIST NUMBER 6

a) How's your staff?
   i) Happy?
   ii) 100% Employed?
   iii) Well paid?
   iv) Have you checked competitive salaries within the last 2 months?
b) How many not so goods are you employing these days?
c) Why don't you fire them?
d) Are you profitable?
   i) Can you take a holiday? If not read chapter 8 again.
   ii) If yes — have you? If not — why don't you?
   If you don't need a break from business — your staff could do with one from you.
e) If you aren't profitable list the actions you are taking to ensure profitability before you next read the checklists.
   i) Put it in your diary to go through the checklists 6 weeks from today.

CHECKLIST NUMBER 7

a) How much work do you do?

b) How much did you do 3 months ago?

c) Therefore how much have you delegated in 3 months?

d) i) How many people have left because they don't have enough responsibility?

   ii) Should you be shedding more?

e) i) Is your business growing?

   ii) If not it's dying. — If you can't fix it better think about starting a new business!

f) Who is the hardest worker in the firm?

g) Who is the most effective worker in the firm?

If you answer to f and g: ME! You have a very high opinion of yourself, do others share it?

If you answer 'someone else' try to learn from them. — And keep them happy.

If f and g are different persons, try to give f and g a bit more of each other, to make them more effective people.

CHECKLIST NUMBER 8

a) How much money have you in the bank?

b) How much do you owe?

c) How much credit is outstanding from credit companies (no-one else I hope!)?

d) How much stock have you?

e) What then is the net worth of the business?

f) How much did you take yesterday?

g) How much did you take last week?

h) What is your stock holding (in week's stock) likely to be at the end of next month. (Using sales forecast).? Is it enough or too much — (it's never just right) — Have you taken any action to get it right?

i) If you cannot answer **all** these questions you'd better start minding your own business before someone has to do it for you.

CHECKLIST NUMBER 9

a) Are you still in charge of all major expenditure?
   Good.
b) And you haven't forgotten those stock shrinkages?
   Good.
c) And honesty is still your policy?
   Good.
d) i) How are you measuring advertising effectiveness?
   ii) Have you sworn not to use a certain method again for a long time?
   iii) Have you submitted a press release within the last month?
      If not — it's time you did.
   iv) What will be your next sales promotion.
      If you don't have one planned you must be happy with just about everything.
e) Are you still walking — or have you learnt to run yet. If you're running how much faster can you go.

CHECKLIST NUMBER 10

a) Are you still selling to almost everyone you meet. Don't stop.
b) Have you had any good ideas recently?
   What did you do with them?
c) Are you still looking for more and more customers?
   Don't stop.
d) i) How many complaints have you received in the last 4 weeks?
   ii) Was it more or less than the previous period?
   iii) What action are you taking to reduce complaints?
   iv) Do you handle every complaint personally?
   If not you could be making a grave mistake. It is this kind of involvement which tells you what's wrong with your business — and you do want to make it perfect — don't you?

CHECKLIST NUMBER 11

For people contemplating buying an existing business.

a) What is it worth to you?
b) Could you do it next door for less?
c) What are they asking for the goodwill?
d) How do you measure the goodwill?
e) Are the customers liable to be loyal to the business?
f) What are the present owners planning to do?
g) Does the character of the business suit your personality (your real personality, not your image of what you'd like to be).
h) What changes will you make?
i) How will these affect the business?
j) How will these affect your family or personal life?

CHECKLIST NUMBER 12

a) How do you measure morale?
b) How's morale in your important areas?
   i) The company staff.
   ii) Your advisers and supporters.
   iii) Your customers.
c) If you're not happy with morale but things are genuinely good.
   See if you can put a bit of zap into your communications.
   Let everyone know what's going on.
   Share a few of your happy secrets.
d) Is everyone doing the job at which he is best?
e) Have you knocked anyone down on a sparkling deal this week?
f) Is it time to sell up yet?